Dynamic Kicks

• ESSENTIALS FOR FREE FIGHTING

Dynamic Kicks

● ESSENTIALS FOR FREE FIGHTING

by CHONG LEE

Graphic Design by Nancy J. Hom

©Ohara Publications, Incorporated 1975
All rights reserved
Printed in the United States of America
Library of Congress Catalog Card Number: 75-36052
Twenty-fourth printing 1995
ISBN 0-89750-017-2

WARNING

OHARA ▉ PUBLICATIONS, INCORPORATED
SANTA CLARITA, CALIFORNIA

Dedication

To all martial artists.

•

——Acknowledgement

My deepest gratitude to H. Eric Hunt for all his help and assistance.

All photographs courtesy of Ron Russo.

●

About the Author

Watching Chong Lee kick is like being hit by waves of energy. He starts loose. Then, imperceptibly, a current begins rushing through his body, building as he picks up speed. Slotting into place, his muscles wrench together in the last microsecond and power literally jolts from the end of his leg. Even from a distance, you can feel it pound the air.

Perhaps what makes Chong Lee's kicking so dynamic is his attitude, both in training and performing. "If people watching can't feel my kick from a distance," he says, "then I've failed. Art inspires emotion in the observer." The exhilaration he inspired while capturing the Forms Grand Championship at the 1974 Long Beach Internationals proved Lee's artistry to everyone there.

Indeed, Chong Lee can kick. He kicks hard and he kicks beautifully, an ability developed only through years of practice. At the tender age of five, young Lee spent every moment he was permitted at a neighborhood dojang studying ji do kwon under one of the leading tae kwon do masters of that time, Chong Byung Wha He seldom played with other boys, considering their games childish. Instead, his world was one of devastating kicks, free-fighting and forms.

At seven, Chong Lee earned his first degree black belt, becoming famous throughout tae kwon do circles as one of the youngest black belts of his day. He was constantly in demand at demonstrations, as much for his impressively refined arsenal of techniques as for his youth.

His fanaticism grew with the coming of maturity and wider renown. At nine, inspired by old Korean martial art movies, he decided to run away from home; his goal — the mountains and the legendary monks who lived there. In time, he realized that the monastery was only a dream. Still, he continued his quest for instructors able to teach him more about the subject that interested him most — full-contact sparring. At the age of eleven, deciding to study more than just tae kwon do, he enrolled in an academy of Thai boxing. There, he learned to fight "tough." He fractured his jaw twice and broke his forearm and toes several times. He persisted, however, for two years, perfecting his skills in this art.

When the opportunity arose that would take him and his entire family to the United States, he quickly seized it. The Chong Lee family settled in California.

In Los Angeles, Lee was introduced to American no-contact karate. With his full-contact background, it took him several years to adjust to this new system. He was constantly being disqualified for facial contact, but trying to repress his attacks only made him lose bouts. Though he did finally learn to adapt his kicks, he now finds himself lingering more in forms and full-contact fighting — a rare combination, but one that suits him handily.

Young and strong, Chong Lee is constantly innovating new, more dynamic kicks. He is one of the few people, for instance, able to throw triple, alternating kicks in midair and, although many lay claim to it, he is one of the few who can truly deliver powerful kicks to almost any angle. Practical kicking is what makes Chong Lee a fighter but what makes him great is, undoubtedly, his creative style.

Preface

Of all the techniques used in the martial arts, perhaps the most difficult to learn and perfect are the kicking techniques. Because many of the muscles used are not stressed in ordinary daily activity, there is great danger of spraining or tearing, especially for beginners. Moreover, without proper limbering and stretching exercises, the martial artist, thinking he will probably never kick well, encounters a good deal of frustration. Also, for most students who find particular difficulty in kicking, it is the method of kicking that needs to be corrected, not the individual's body structure.

Still, in spite of all these variables, there are basic physical laws, built on certain anatomical similarities in all men, which govern the movements of would-be kickers. All men have two legs that function in certain ways and there exist standard principles for making these legs work most efficiently and most powerfully. Rather than cover all the variables, this text hopes to delineate the essence of the more popular kicks evolved out of the last five to seven years of free-fighting, and thereby, clarify these basic physical laws and standard principles.

Chong Lee, known as one of the country's top kicking specialists, presents the ideal opportunity to study virtually perfect kicking motion. However, please remember that all the kicks Chong

Lee demonstrates are photographed in their extremes. Kicks, for instance, are not always thrown high and to the head, but the theory here is that the head is the most difficult target, being the farthest from the feet. And, if a martial artist has the capability of controlled motion to the head, the lower targets are that much more accessible. This principle obviously does not work in reverse. The idea of proficient kicking is to be able to deliver power to any target that is beyond the range of one's hands.

Chong Lee's kicks present a series of exacting movements that can provide power to a person of average anatomical structure—if he takes the time to develop himself. Variations can make the kicks more practical for individual differences in build, even if these variations decrease the kicks' total power. Experiment.

Contents

Stretching Exercises

The entire repertoire of stretching exercises alone could fill a book. Consequently, only the major stretches will be discussed here. The most important thing to remember is to move *slowly*. *Feel* the muscles you are trying to stretch and pull against them gently.

Keeping the body loose for extended periods of time is also very important. It does not help to stretch only once a week or once every three days. In the beginning, the student should attempt to hold each position for as long as possible, repeating the stretches every three or four hours, *every day*.

Before starting each training session, the joints in the entire body should be loosened by manipulation. Extra time should be devoted to loosening the hip, knee and ankle joints.

After the stretching exercises and before working out, perform your kicking motions slowly, gradually working up to full power.

KNEE BENDS

(1) Straighten your legs, putting your feet together, and bend over, placing your hands on the fronts of your knees. (2) With your hands still on your knees, squat fully and balance on the balls of your feet. (3) Straighten up again while pushing your knees back into the straight locked position. Repeat at least ten times.

STANDING BODY FOLD

(1) Straighten your legs, put your feet together and bend over, placing your hands on the sides of your knees. (2) Sliding them down your legs, use your hands to pull and fold your body forward at the hips. (3) Double over so that your head is as close to your shins as possible. Remember to keep your legs straight. Hold this position for as long as you can. Release, straighten up and stand erect. Repeat this exercise until your lower back and thigh muscles are relaxed.

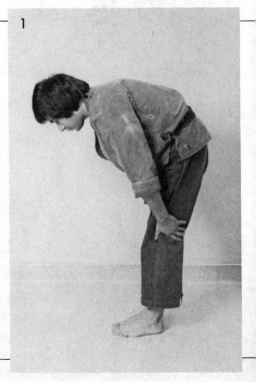

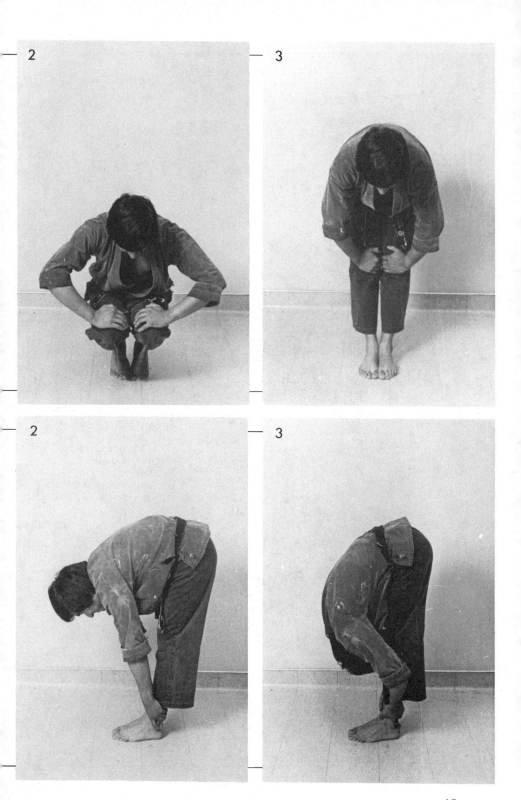

SQUATTING STRETCH

(1) Squat on your right leg, extend your left leg straight out to the side with your knee locked. Bend forward at the waist. (2) Squat on your left leg, extend your right leg straight out to the side with your knee locked and repeat the exercise. Alternate right and left legs until your back and leg muscles are relaxed.

SINGLE LEG SITTING STRETCH

(1) Sit on the floor with your right leg extended, knee locked straight. Bend your left leg, placing your left foot on top of your right thigh. Grab your right foot or right leg below the knee and pull your head and chest down toward your right shin. If possible, touch your nose to your knee. Hold this position for as long as you can. (2) Do the same exercise with your left leg extended and right leg bent. Repeat stretching each leg until the backs of your legs are relaxed.

DOUBLE STRAIGHT-LEG SITTING STRETCH

(1) Sit on the floor with both legs straight, knees locked, and spread them as far to the sides as possible. Bend straight forward from your hips, lowering your chest and head as close to the floor as possible. Hold this position for about a minute.

DOUBLE STRAIGHT-LEG SPLITS STRETCH

(1) Lower yourself as far as possible into a straight split—left leg in front, right leg in back. Tighten the inside muscles of your legs as if you were going to rise out of the split by pulling your legs together. Then, relax your muscles to lower yourself farther into the split. Alternate tensing and relaxing your muscles to lower yourself to the ground. (2) Turn your body around, putting your right leg in front and your left leg in back. Repeat the exercise.

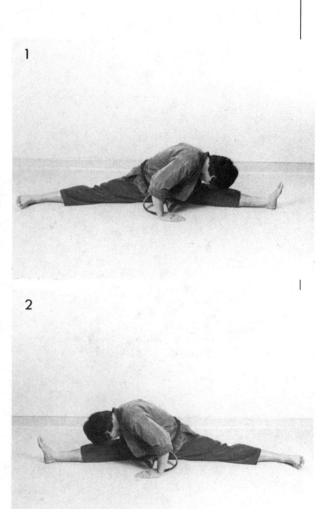

1

2

DOUBLE BENT-LEG SITTING STRETCH

(1) Sit on the floor with both legs bent and the soles of your feet pressed together. Spread your knees as far as possible, grab your feet with both hands and pull your forehead to your feet. Hold this position for about a minute.

BALANCING SIDE KICK STRETCH

(1) Balance on your left leg. Lift your right leg up, knee bent, while grasping the back of your right calf with your right hand. (2) Slowly straighten your right leg while turning your right hip forward. Hold your leg up with your right hand. Do the same exercise with your left leg. Eventually, you should be able to perform this holding or "lock out" exercise without the aid of your hand.

Techniques Basic to All Kicks

As noted earlier, certain standard principles—based on the laws of physics and the human anatomy—exist to guide all kickers in the most efficient and most powerful use of their legs. The judicious student practices, religiously, certain techniques based on these principles, whether he delivers a roundhouse kick or a side kick, a front kick or a hook kick, because he realizes that they apply to almost all kicking executions.

The following five precepts are by no means the entire range of techniques basic to all kicking. They do present, however, the more important aspects of kicking movement. Of these five precepts, the first three—using full power only at full extension; raising the kicking knee and leg up high and maintaining a straight line through the body, hips and legs—should be given the utmost consideration.

FIG. I

KICK POWER   REACTION POWER

Top View of Man Kicking Against Wall
Body, Hips and Leg Not Aligned

FIG. II

KICK POWER   REACTION POWER

Top View of Man Kicking Against Wall
Body, Hips and Leg Aligned

● *Use full power only at full extension.* Many practitioners use full power throughout execution of a technique and, as a result, they must tense their muscles continuously. This tension not only hinders speed of execution but also wastes power. While all kicks should be executed at maximum speed, the entire leg should remain relaxed until the point of full extension. Then, complete power (and by consequence, muscle tension) should be applied in one short, swift burst.

● *Raise the kicking knee and leg up high.* All kicks should be initiated with the knee raised as high as possible, poised for speedy flexing (see no. 1). Execution can then follow in one smooth motion, with the leg extending as is appropriate for the specific kick involved.

This upraised position is most favorable because:

(a) Kicks exert greater penetrating power when the angle between the extending leg and a line running horizontally through the target is decreased.

(b) It gives your opponent less time to react: with the knee raised high, the kick can shoot out to a wider range of targets (high, medium, low). As a result, it becomes increasingly difficult for the opponent to anticipate quickly the kick's ultimate target.

(c) A kick initiated from this position is harder to block. When the kick is driven up from the ground directly to the target, the opponent need only lower his forearm to counter the blow. With the leg raised high and closer to the opponent's body, he cannot block with such simple effectiveness. He cannot readily anticipate the line traveled by the extending leg and, consequently, cannot rapidly decide on a suitable block.

In conjunction with the above, the wise fighter never begins by bringing his kicking foot back to the knee of his supporting leg (see no. 2). This sort of movement diminishes speed and wastes power. For example, consider the fighter faced with an opponent's approaching head punch. He spots an opening to the opponent's rib cage and, hoping to deliver a side kick before the punch lands, cocks his foot back to the knee of his supporting leg. At this point, he begins to appreciate the stupidity of this initial move. Before he can raise his knee and execute the kick, the opponent's punch connects. The fighter should have raised the knee of his kicking leg while thrusting the side kick forward. Then, even if his kick was too slow to land effectively in and of itself, the opponent's advance would have been stopped and his punch nullified.

● *Maintain a straight line through the body, hips and legs.*

(a) Power and speed are primary qualities of strong, solid kicks. However, if only the leg muscles work to execute the kick, power and speed are generated by these muscles alone (see no. 3).

On the other hand, when the hips are also thrust forward in line with the extending leg (see no. 4), the whole body contributes to the force of the kick. The thrust created by using the hip multiplies the speed of the leg and a tremendous amount of power results.

(b) In addition, even if the hip is thrown in the same direction as the extending leg, power and speed are drastically reduced unless the body follows in this line also. For example, assume that in a side kick delivered to a brick wall, the hip and extending leg are in line but the body is not (see no. 5 and figure I). The brick wall is immovable so the force of the kick is redirected back toward the kicker. At this point, the body and leg function as separate units connected by the hip joint: the extended leg moves back with the redirected thrust. This force is absorbed by a backward spring in the hip joint but the body still continues its movement forward. In the end, total power is lost as it is diverted along several different directional lines—some of these moving away from the intended target. Also, the varying lines of force work against each other, diminishing speed.

If, on the other hand, the body, hip and extending leg are held on the same line (see no. 6 and figure II), all move in one direction—either through the wall (breaking either the wall or the kicker's foot) or away from it in the opposite direction. In both cases, the power and speed generated are not diverted but move in one line. Power and speed here may be redirected altogether but neither is diminished, divided or reduced.

● *Keep sudden changes in rhythm and movement to a minimum.*
Before and during initiation of any kicking technique, the fighter's eyes and body should not undergo any sudden, discernable change. If, while free-fighting, his body constantly moves, this movement should be maintained for as long as possible before the actual kick begins. If, however, the fighter's stance is rigid and without movement, his body should be kept perfectly still and only the leg should move (albeit, very swiftly) at the start of the

kick. The point here, in any case, is keeping the opponent from obtaining any foreknowledge of an upcoming kick.

● *Use eye feints and peripheral vision.* Because eyes (quick glances, visual preoccupations, etc.) often betray a fighter's upcoming targets, noting the opponent's eye movements can provide clues to his immediate intentions. The clever fighter, then, watches his opponent's eyes but uses eye feints to disguise his own intentions. He also uses peripheral vision as much as focused eyesight since this gives him a wider range of visual awareness. Narrowly focused eyesight, on the other hand, necessarily leads the fighter to concentrate on only one area at a time, causing him to neglect other spots open to attack.

Striking Areas of the Foot

There are five basic striking areas of the foot: (1) the heel, (2) the ball, (3) the arch, (4) the instep and (5) the outside edge. Heel strikes land with either the bottom of the heel or the back of the heel. In both cases, pull your toes and instep up toward your knee to allow the heel to make primary contact. To hit with the ball of your foot, however, point your instep but pull your toes back toward your knee. This position allows the ball of your foot to make primary contact. Kicks landing with the arch of your foot (the area between the heel and the ball) may be executed with your foot pointed slightly (in sweeps, for example) or angled up toward the knee (as in side kicks and stomps). To hit with your instep (the bony area on top between the ankle and toes), point your foot slightly, curling your toes a little. Kicks hitting with the outside edge of your foot (from heel to ball) are executed with the arch curved inward toward your knee to allow the outside edge of your foot to make primary contact.

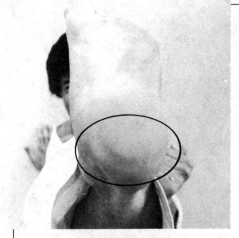

HEEL

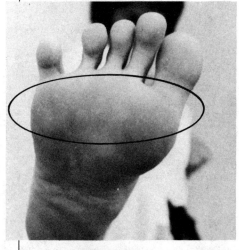

BALL

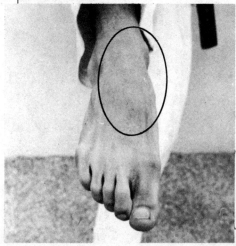

INSTEP

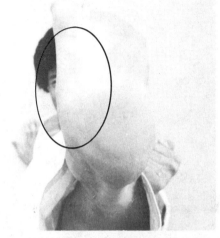

ARCH

OUTSIDE EDGE

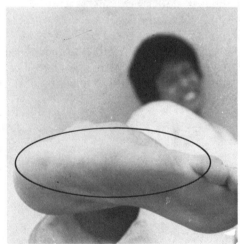

Dynamic Kicks

Read the step-by-step explanations as you study the general motions presented in the photographs. Run through the entire kick softly, concentrating on each individual movement until you can *feel* that movement. When you can feel the motion, proceed to the next step. Go through the entire kick this way, paying special attention to the muscles tensed at the kick's full extension.

1

4

BASIC FRONT KICK

(1) Begin with your left foot forward. (2) Twist your upper body to the left as if throwing a right punch. (3&4) Use this momentum to move your right knee forward and lift it high to the right side of your chest. As it comes up, it should brush closely against your supporting left leg. (5) As your right leg extends, tighten the muscles of your supporting leg and turn your right hip forward. (6) *At full extension, the muscles on the right side of your stomach and the back of your supporting leg are fully tensed.* (7-10) Release your tension and use your hips to pull your right leg back to your original stance.

8

1

4

7

SLIDING FRONT KICK

(1) Begin with your right foot forward and much of your weight on your left leg. (2&3) Draw your right foot up and forward in an arcing motion so that your right knee seems to rush toward the right side of your chest. This should start your sliding motion. (4) Time full extension to occur with the end of your slide. *The right side of your stomach and high backside of your supporting leg are completely tensed, as are the calf muscles of your kicking leg.* (5-8) As your right leg lowers, hop off it and return to your original stance.

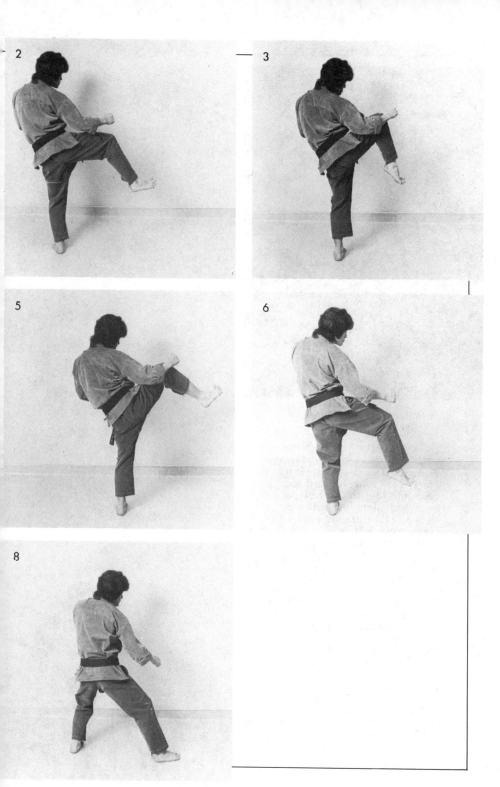

JUMPING FRONT KICK (FORWARD FOOT)

(1) Begin with your right foot forward and most of your weight on your left leg. (2&3) Shift your weight to your forward leg, scoop your left foot in front of your right knee and jump off with your right leg so that it passes your left foot again. Your left foot is touching an invisible step. (4) Led by your right hip, your right leg continues and thrusts to full extension. In form, the lower leg (in this case, the left leg) is held in a cocked position as the lead photo shows. In competition, however, it is a good idea to extend the non-kicking foot toward the floor as demonstrated here in the step-by-step sequence. This safeguards against being irretrievably upset while in the air. *At full extension, your entire right leg and the right side of your lower back are completely tensed.* (5) As the tension releases, drop onto your left leg. (6&7) Lower your right foot to assume your original stance.

1

4

7

JUMPING FRONT KICK
(REAR FOOT)

(1) Begin with your right foot forward and most of your weight on your left leg. (2) As your right knee lifts, push off with your left leg. (3) Relax in the air and place your right foot lightly on an invisible step. (4) As your left hand and shoulder turn to the right, thrust your left hip in the same direction and begin extending your kick. (5) *At full extension, your entire left leg and the left side of your lower back are completely tensed.* (6&7) Pull your upper body back to land on your right leg. (8&9) Lower your kicking leg into a left stance.

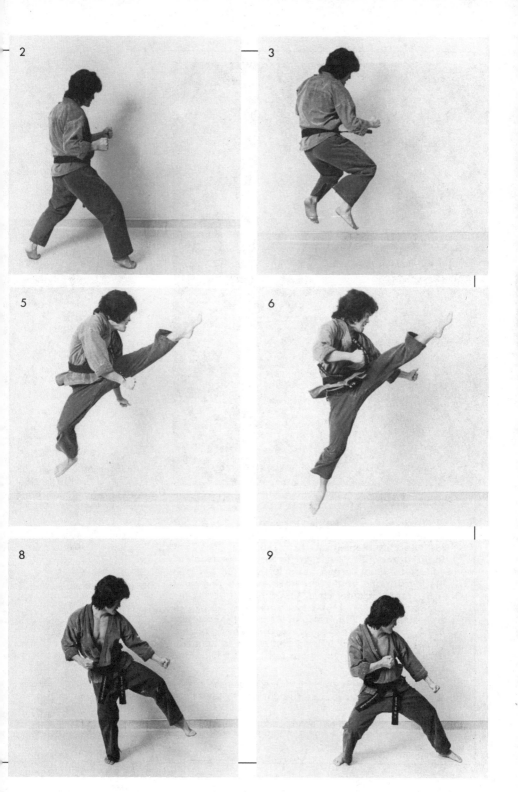

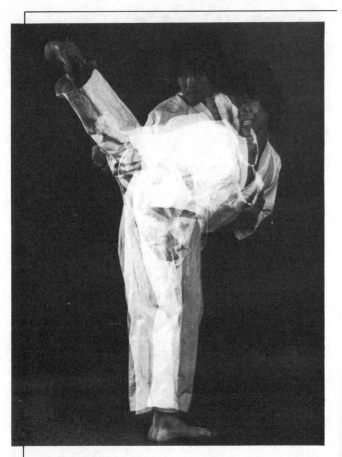

BASIC SIDE KICK

(1) Begin with your left leg forward. (2) Twist your upper body to the left as if throwing a right punch. (3) Use this momentum to move your right foot forward and lift your right knee high in front of you. (4-6) Pivot further to the left on your supporting leg, turning your right knee over so that your right foot, leading edge first, may continue its straight path. (7) *At full extension, the muscles in your right leg and the entire right side of your lower back and buttocks are completely tensed.* (8-13) Release your tension and return to your original stance by bringing your right foot back along the same path.

It is important that your kicking foot does not travel in an arc but moves in a straight line to the target (see inset).

SLIDING SIDE KICK

(1) Begin with your right foot forward and most of your weight on your left leg. (2) Shifting your weight as little as possible, lift your right knee up high to the right side of your body. (3 & 4) Shoot your kick out straight to the side, leading with the edge of your right foot. The momentum of the lift and kick, done in a single motion, will slide you toward your target. Be sure to hold the edge of your right foot parallel to the ground. (5) *At full extension, the muscles in your right leg and the entire right side of your lower back and buttocks are completely tensed.* (6—9) Release your tension and simply drop your right leg back into your original stance.

Again, a major concern is bringing your right foot up and out in a straight line, without arcing.

JUMPING SIDE KICK

(1) Begin with your right foot forward, weight evenly distributed. (2) Pushing on it slightly, skip your left foot toward your right. At the same time, jump off with your right leg. (3) As you rise, cock both legs—your right leg up near your body, your left slightly below your right. (4&5) At the peak of your jump, shoot your right leg out horizontally. *At full extension, the right side of your lower back and your right buttock are completely tensed, with the bottom of your left foot turning upward tightly.* (6-8) As your right leg pops back into its cocked position, your left leg extends downward to touch the floor. Keep your right hand held high and your left hand ready to punch. (9&10) As your left foot touches the floor, lower your right leg and return to your original stance.

1

4

7

JUMPING BACK SIDE KICK

(1) Begin in a left foot forward stance with most of your weight resting on your rear leg. (2) Leading with your right elbow and hip, start a clockwise spin. Your left heel should come up off the floor as you turn. (3&4) Still spinning, shift your weight to your left foot; then, jump off it. Cock your left foot up beneath you as your right knee lifts up high. (5) As your body continues its clockwise movement, extend your right leg horizontally, hitting with the back of your right heel. *At full extension, the entire right side of your back and right leg are fully tensed.* (6) As your right leg begins returning to your body, twist your right hip down and to the back. (7) Simultaneously, extend your left leg to touch the floor. (8&9) As you land on your left leg, lower your right to the floor in front of you.

DEFENSE COUNTER SIDE KICK

(1) Begin in a right foot forward stance with most of your weight resting on your rear leg. (2&3) Shift your weight to your left leg and jump backwards off both feet. As you rise, cock your right leg horizontally to the side, bring your right knee up as high as possible and pull your right foot back. Cock your left foot beneath you, turning its sole upward. (4) At the peak of your jump, lean forward and begin extending your right leg horizontally. (5) *At full extension, the right side of your back is tightly arched and your right heel is turned upward slightly.* (6) As your right leg returns, twist your right hip down and back. Simultaneously, extend your left leg to touch the floor. (7-9) When your left leg lands, lower your right leg to the floor in front of you.

SPIN BACK SIDE KICK

(1) Begin with your left foot forward. (2&3) With most of your weight on your right leg, pivot clockwise 180 degrees and snap your head around over your right shoulder to watch the target. As you pivot, your left heel should come up and turn toward the target. (4&5) Shift your weight to your left leg. In one motion, continue pivoting on your left foot as your right leg, led by your right foot and hip, comes around and back. Smoothly fire your kick in a straight line to the target. (6) *At full extension, the muscles in your right leg and the entire right side of your lower back and buttocks are completely tensed.* (7&8) Release your tension and allow your right leg to spring back into a cocked position. (9&10) Lower your right foot to the floor in front of you.

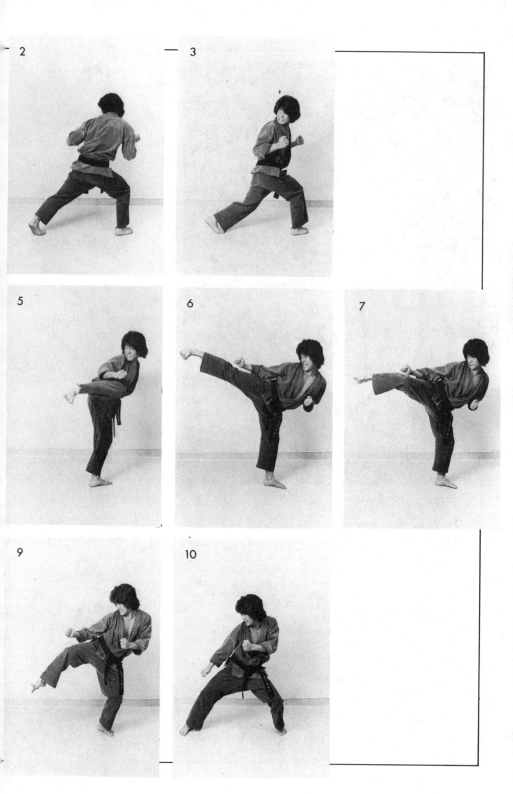

1

5

9

FRONT HOOK KICK

(1) Begin with your right foot forward. (2) Turning your right hip and shoulder forward in front of you, begin lifting your right leg. (3&4) Bring your right knee up high toward the right side of your chest. (5) As you do so, pivot counterclockwise on your supporting leg while turning the bottom of your right foot toward the target. As in all hook kicks, your kicking foot should come up in an arcing motion. (6&7) As your right leg extends, jerk your right hip and shoulder to the right so that your foot travels up and across in a continuation of its arc. (8) *The point of full extension occurs with a hooking motion in which the back of your right leg and the right side of your lower back are tensed and slowly pulling against the extension of the kick.* (9) Continue this powerful, snapping hook until your leg is tucked back in a cocked position. At this point, your right foot should still be tensed. (10-12) Drop your right foot immediately into your original stance.

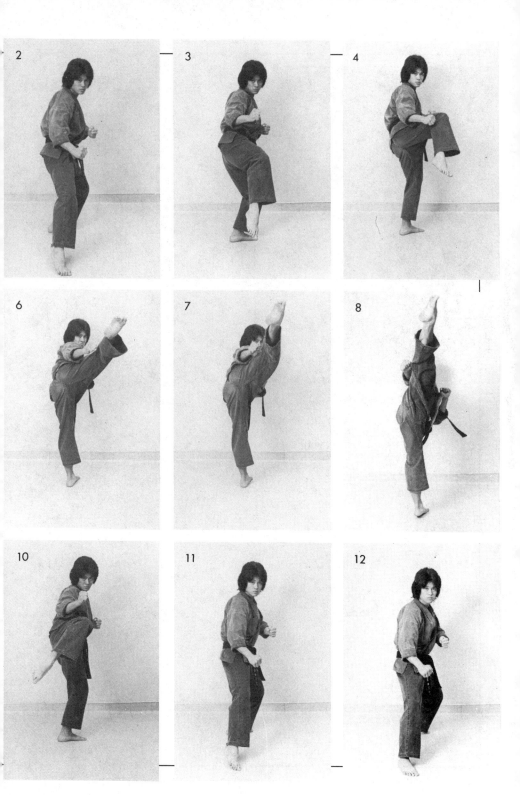

SLIDING HOOK KICK

(1) Begin with your right foot forward and most of your weight on your left leg. (2) Bring your right leg upward to kick in an outward, arcing motion. (3-5) Use the momentum of this movement to lift and slide yourself forward. (6) *Near full extension, jerk your right hip and shoulder to the right. Tense the back of your right leg and the right side of your lower back to achieve the powerful whipping hook.* (7) Keep your right foot tense as it continues its motion, snapping it back to a cocked position. (8&9) Lower your right foot directly in front of you to return to your original stance.

1

3

7

11

JUMPING FRONT HOOK KICK

(1) Begin with your right foot forward. (2&3) Push slightly with your left leg and, as your left foot skips toward your right, jump off with your right leg. (4) Tucking your left foot up beneath you, cock your right leg near the right side of your chest—high and parallel to the ground. (5-8) Extend your right leg upward in a circular arc while arching your back. Drop your right shoulder backwards to hook your kick across. (9) *Near full extension of your kick, your left leg should be reaching for the ground.* (10) Land on your left leg as your right leg retracts. (11&12) Then, lower your right leg to your original stance.

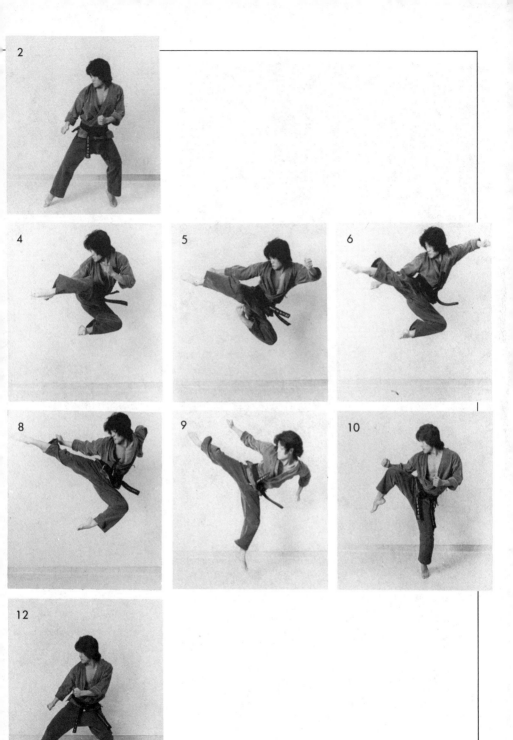

SPIN BACK HOOK KICK

(1) Begin with your left foot forward. (2) With your weight on your right foot, turn clockwise 180 degrees, pivoting so that the heel of your left foot comes off the ground and turns toward the target. (3) As you shift your weight onto your left leg, snap your head around over your right shoulder to look at your opponent. Start moving your right foot toward the target. (4-6) Lead with your right foot in a tight, hooking motion, arcing your right knee up past your chest. (7) *At full extension, the right side of your lower back is tightly arched and the back of your right leg is pulling against the centrifugal force of your extending leg.* (8&9) Relax your tension and allow the momentum of your right foot to bend your right knee. (10&11) Drop your right foot to the floor in front of you.

1

5

9

13

BACK HOOK KICK, STEPPING AWAY

(1) Begin with your left foot forward. (2) While watching your target over your left shoulder, pivot your body clockwise and step away with your right foot. (3) Draw your left foot toward your right to take another step. (4) As you plant your left foot in front of your right, shift your weight to your left leg. Snap your head around to look back over your right shoulder. (5-7) Lift your right foot in an arcing motion by bringing your right knee close to the right side of your chest while keeping your foot turned toward the target. (8&9) *Extend your kick in a hooking motion by snapping your right leg straight out and tightly arching the right side of your lower back. The muscles in the back of your kicking leg should be pulling against the centrifugal force of your extending kick.* (10-15) Past the kick's full extension, allow your right knee to bend, using the arched position of your back and the momentum of your returning foot to draw the right side of your body down and back. This should return you to your original stance.

JUMPING BACK HOOK KICK

(1) Begin with your left foot forward. (2&3) Jump off both feet, using your upper torso to spin your body clockwise. (4) As you turn, keep your knees bent and your feet tucked up. (5) As your right side nears your target, extend your right leg in a snapping motion. (6) *At full extension, your right foot is tensed and the right side of your back is arched tightly.* (7&8) Just past or during extension, allow your left foot to drift down to the floor. (9&10) As your left foot touches the floor, your kick should have expended itself. Allow your right knee to bend in retraction. (11-13) Let your momentum continue and complete the turn by dropping your right leg down and back into your original stance.

OUTSIDE CRESCENT KICK

(1) Begin with your right foot forward. (2&3) Step forward with your left foot. (4) Shoot your right hip and leg across and in front of your left foot. (5&6) Kick your right leg up across your body with your knee leading your foot in a wide arc. (7) *At full extension, the right side of your stomach is tight. Your right foot should move across the center line as your right thigh pushes outward and your right hip starts back. Your fully extended kick should travel across on a horizontal line.* (8-10) After your foot passes the center, draw it down and back in a slight arc, settling into a left stance.

The initial step or shuffle creates an opening for drawing the opponent's attack. The kick, then, catches him while he is coming in. The kick may be executed without the step.

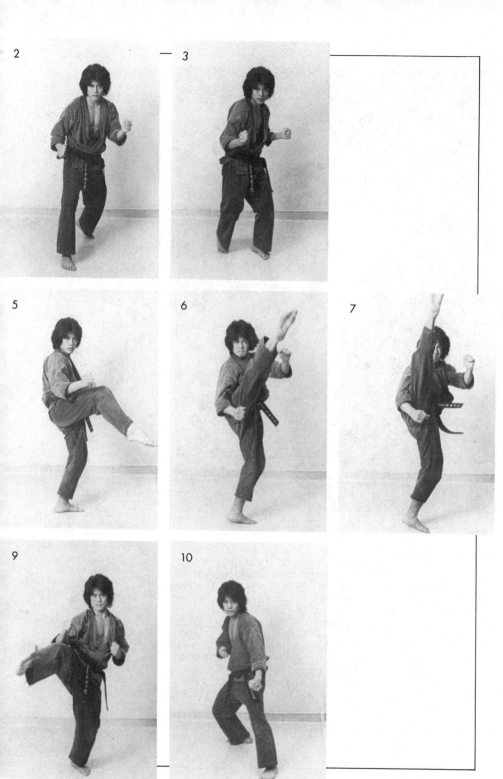

INSIDE CRESCENT KICK

8

(1) Begin with your left foot forward. (2) Twist your upper body to the left as if throwing a right punch. (3&4) Use this momentum to kick your leg high up toward the right side of your chest while thrusting your right hip forward. (5) *Full extension should begin just right of the center line and move to the middle as you tighten the calf and lower thigh of your kicking leg. The right side of your stomach should be tight also.* (6-9) Use all the muscles in the back of your right leg and the top of your left thigh to slam your right leg straight down, loosening them again just as you settle into a right stance.

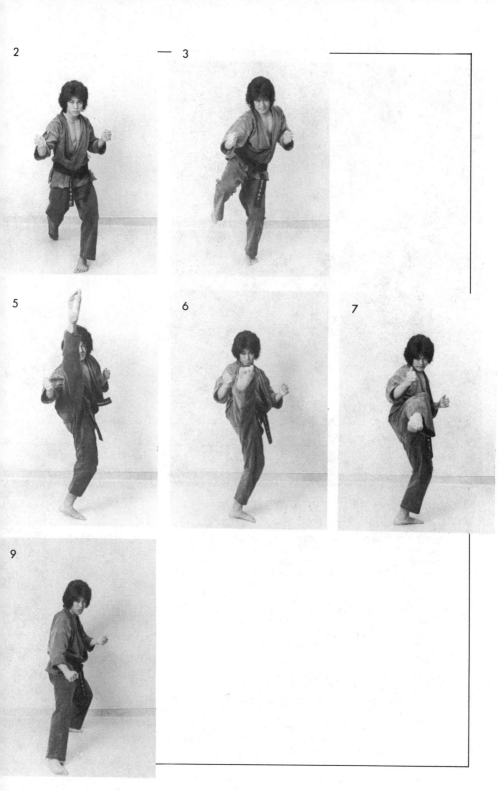

2

3

5

6

7

9

1

5

9

JUMPING OUTSIDE CRESCENT KICK

(1) Begin with your right foot forward and much of your weight resting on your rear leg. (2) Shift your weight to your right leg. (3-5) Skip your left foot forward and jump off your right foot, bringing your right leg up in front of you in a clockwise arc. (6) *At full extension, your left foot reaches for the ground again while your right foot reaches up and out. The muscles in your neck and the right side of your stomach are tensed to keep your weight behind the kick.* (7-11) Relax as your kick continues its circular course, dropping down again into a right stance.

Again, the outside crescent kick, jumping or otherwise, may be varied by emphasizing a hard, straight, downward motion once the kick has reached the center line.

The Thai kicking variation may also be used. Making certain that the kick travels in a full horizontal motion upon impact offers maximum power.

SPIN BACK OUTSIDE CRESCENT KICK

(1) Begin with your left foot forward. (2&3) With your weight on your right foot, turn clockwise 180 degrees and look over your right shoulder. The heel of your left foot should come off the ground and turn toward the target as you pivot. (4-6) Shift your weight to your left foot and continue turning: first your shoulders, hips and then your leg. As your right leg lifts and straightens, bend forward at the waist, dropping your right hip down. (7) *At full extension, your kicking foot is tensed but your body is loose and striving for maximum speed as the four moving parts blend together.* For maximum power, your foot should be traveling on a line running horizontally to the target. (8-10) Relax as your kick continues its circular course and drop down into a right stance.

1

5

JUMPING SPIN BACK OUTSIDE CRESCENT KICK

(1) Begin with your left foot forward. (2-4) With your weight on your right foot, turn clockwise 180 degrees and look over your right shoulder. The heel of your left foot should come off the ground and turn toward the target as you pivot. (5&6) Shift your weight to your left foot and, as you jump off it, snap your right shoulder, hip and then leg, around, straightening your kicking leg as it sweeps across in front of you. (7&8) *Full extension occurs on a horizontal line in front of you. Your right foot and the outside of your kicking leg should be tensed as your leg sweeps across. Your stomach, too, wrenches down to pull your weight forward into the kick.* (9&10) Either during or past the kick's extension, drop your left leg down to touch the floor. Arch your back to keep your body erect. (11&12) Bend your right leg and allow it to swing freely back to its original position.

9

3

7

BASIC FULL ROUNDHOUSE KICK

(1) Begin with your left foot forward. (2&3) Twist your upper body to the left as if throwing a right punch, lifting your right knee to the side. (4-6) Swing your knee and foot forward in an arcing motion, extending your leg to the target when your shin becomes parallel to the floor and is centered across your right hand and shoulder line. (7) As your leg extends, turn your right shoulder back and arch your back. This counter-torquing motion feeds a final burst of power to the end of your kick. *At full extension, the muscles in your stomach and the entire right side of your back are fully tensed.* (8-10) Retract your leg along the same path, moving your right foot back to return to your original stance.

In contrast to a side kick's straight line of delivery and a hook kick's rising swoop, the roundhouse kick is delivered in a forward arc which begins with an upraised position of the knee (see inset).

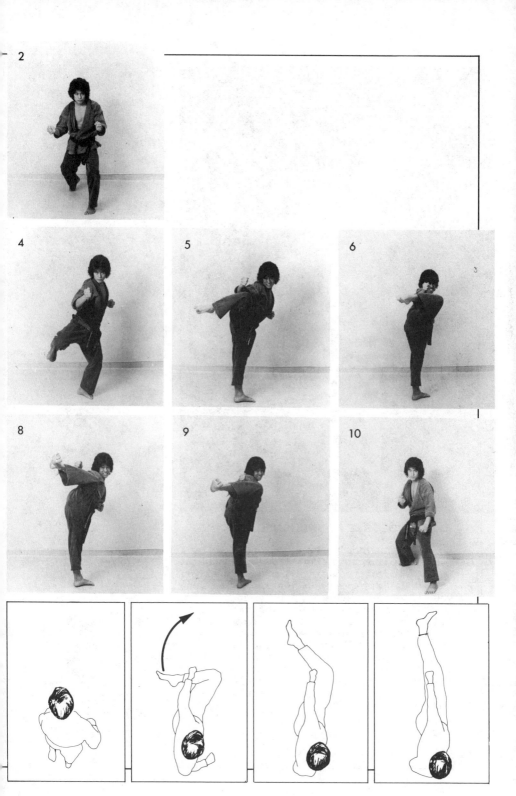

BASIC 30-DEGREE ROUNDHOUSE KICK

(1) Begin with your left foot forward. (2&3) Twist your upper body to the left as if throwing a right punch. (4) Move your right hip forward as you bring your right knee up in front of you, brushing your right foot closely past your left leg. (5-7) Keeping your knee high, twist your right hip to the left and down in a snapping motion as you extend your leg, arch your back and bring your foot up in an arc. *At full extension, the muscles in your right leg are tensed and the right side of your back is arched tightly.* Turn your face over your right shoulder. (8-12) Release your energy and retract your leg along the same path, returning to your original stance.

1

4

SLIDING ROUNDHOUSE KICK

(1) Begin with your right foot forward, your right leg bent and most of your weight on your left leg. (2-4) Without cocking your leg, lift your right foot in a roundhouse arc as you twist your right hip downward to the left. (5) *At full extension, the right side of your back is tightly arched and your face is turned over your right shoulder. All your momentum is cast into the instep of your supporting foot.* (6-10) When the focus of your kick is spent, allow the elasticity of your body to draw your leg back, simply lowering your foot to the floor.

8

1

4

8

ROUNDHOUSE KICK, STEPPING FORWARD

(1) Begin with your right foot forward. Hold your right fist fairly close to your body. (2&3) Shoot your right fist out in either a fake or an actual back knuckle strike. Use this momentum to pull your left leg forward. (4) Shift your weight to your left leg as your fist returns and begin your kick. (5&6) Bring your right foot up and forward in an arc and drop your right elbow back as your right hand whips across. (7) *You are counter-torqued at full extension so that the right side of your back is tightly arched and your right leg is tensed as well.* (8-10) Release your tension and drop your right leg back into your original stance.

1

4

7

ROUNDHOUSE KICK, JUMPING FORWARD

(1) Begin with your right foot forward. (2) Keeping your left leg to the rear, jump forward off your right foot. Punch upward with your left hand, adding momentum to your jump. (3&4) Hesitate slightly at the height of your jump. Then, jerk your left hand back as your left hip rolls forward and your leg extends. (5) *At full extension, the muscles in your left lower back and both legs are completely tensed.* (6&7) As your left leg retracts, land on your right leg. (8) Lower your left leg into a left foot forward stance.

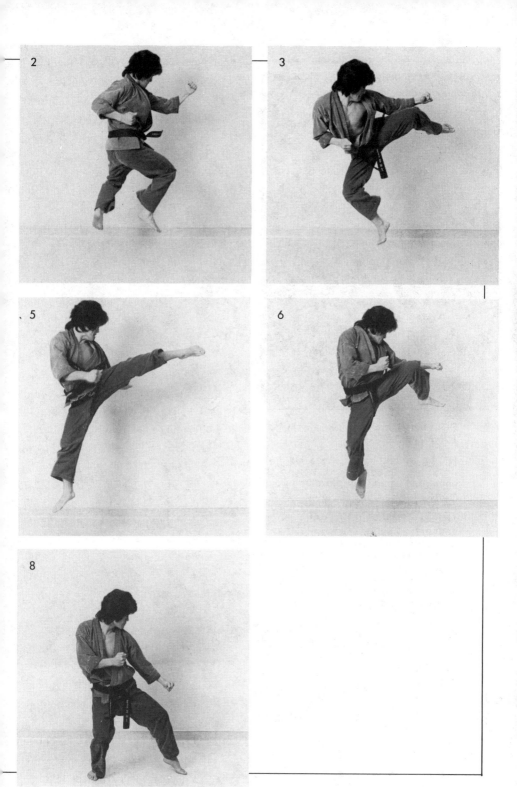

1

4

7

ROUNDHOUSE KICK, JUMPING BACK

(1) Begin with your right leg forward. (2&3) Shift your weight to your rear leg and jump, pulling your right foot and shoulder back. (4) Your left leg travels across and extends. Near full extension, pull your left shoulder back. (5) *At full extension, the muscles in your left lower back and both legs are completely tensed.* (6&7) As your left leg retracts, land on your right leg. (8) Lower your left leg into a left foot forward stance.

This is strictly a defensive kick. Jump back just enough to clear full extension of your opponent's attack, but stay close enough to reach him with the kick.

SPIN BACK ROUNDHOUSE KICK

(1) Begin with your left foot forward and most of your weight on your right leg. (2&3) Keeping your weight on your right foot, lead with your shoulders and snap your head around clockwise 360 degrees. (4) Now, shifting your weight to your left leg, brush your right foot close to your stationary leg and swing your knee and right hip forward. (5-7) Keeping your right knee high, extend your foot in an upward arc. (8) *At full extension, the muscles in your right leg are tensed and the right side of your back is tightly arched.* (9&10) Release your tension and retract your leg to the cocked position. (11&12) Lower your right foot gently to the ground in front of you.

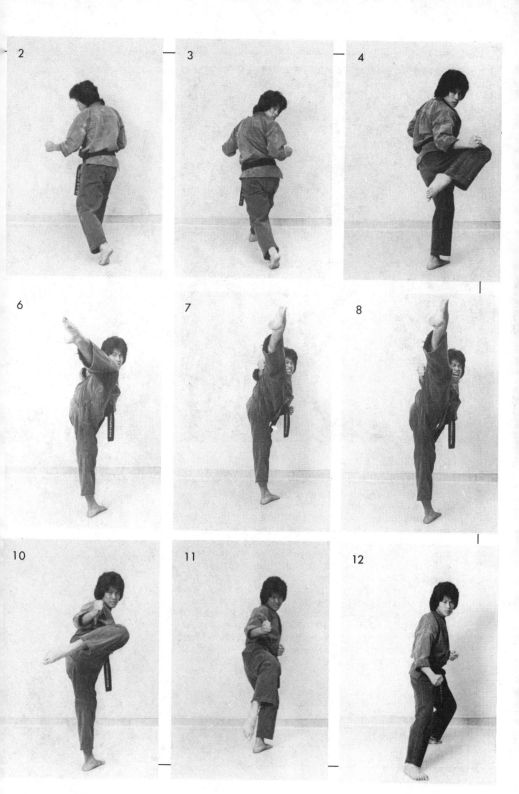

1

4

8

DROP SIDE KICK

(1) Begin with your right leg forward. (2&3) Lean back over your left leg and drop your hands to the floor while watching over your right shoulder. At the same time, cock your right knee up near your right shoulder. You should be supporting yourself on your hands, your left knee and the ball of that foot. (4) Fire the side kick, making sure that your right foot travels in a straight line. (5) *At full extension, your shoulders, the muscles in your right leg and the entire right side of your lower back and buttocks are completely tensed.* Your weight is centered primarily on your hands and the ball of your left foot. (6-10) Release your tension, allowing your right leg to lower itself. Shift your weight forward and push off on your left leg, rising back into your original stance.

DROP ROUNDHOUSE KICK

(1) Begin with your right foot forward. (2&3) Turn back over your left knee and jerk your right knee up as you drop to your hands. You should land in a tripod, using your hands and left foot as support. (4&5) Leading with your right knee, extend your roundhouse kick upward. (6) *At full extension, your lower right back and right leg are completely tensed, as are both your shoulders. Your hands are pushing hard against the floor.* (7) Release the tension in your right leg and (8) retract your kick. (9-11) Set your right foot down and draw your left knee up to your chest. (12&13) Raise yourself up into a right stance.

1

5

9

DROP SPIN KICK

(1) Begin with your left foot forward. (2) Shifting most of your weight to your right leg, pivot clockwise 180 degrees while watching your target over your left shoulder. (3&4) Drop to the ground on your left knee, placing your left hand on the floor in front of your right foot. Snap your head around to look back over your right shoulder. (5) Jerk your left knee forward while extending your right leg in a clockwise arc. The instant your right leg goes out, drop your right hand to the floor. Support yourself on both hands, your left knee and the ball of that foot. (6&7) *During full extension of the kick, your right buttock is completely tensed.* (8&9) As your right leg continues its arc, bend that knee and place the ball of your right foot on the floor behind you. Your left knee should begin to come off the floor. (10-12) Using this momentum and your left hand for assistance, lean forward and rise into your original stance. The swinging of your right hand from its position on the floor to the right side of your body should give you extra lift.

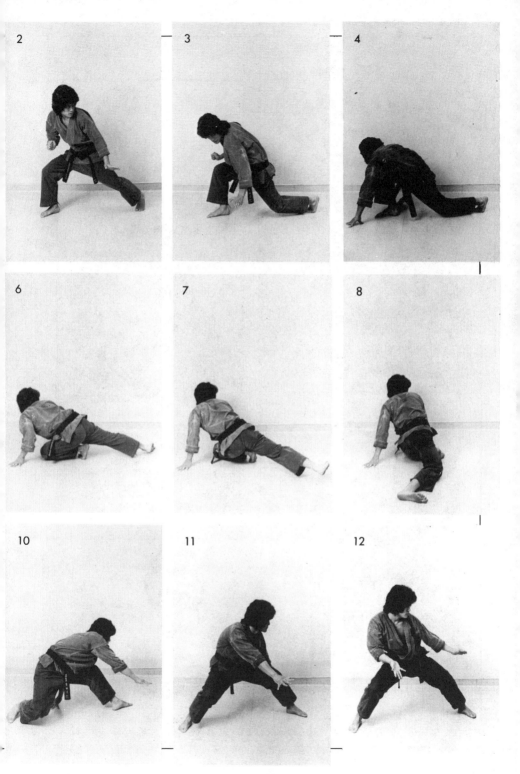

Some people have scrapbooks filled with notes and souvenirs. Chong Lee's is crammed with random snapshots of him working out, trying new techniques or perfecting older ones. He is seldom at rest; his energy doesn't let him.

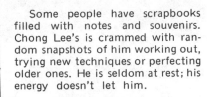